The Snake Pyjamas

Contents

How to use the *Rigby Navigator Poetry* Teaching Guides.......... 2

Renewed Framework Teaching Objectives 3

Lesson 1 6

Lesson 2 7

Lesson 3 8

Lesson 4 9

PCM 1 10

PCM 2 11

Lesson 5 12

Lesson 6 13

Lesson 7 14

Lesson 8 15

PCM 3 16

PCM 4 17

Lesson 9 18

Lesson 10 19

Lesson 11 20

Lesson 12 21

PCM 5 22

PCM 6 23

How to use the Rigby Navigator Poetry Teaching Guides

The *Navigator* Teaching Guides offer flexible routes through the poetry books for guided reading. The Guides put you in control of guided reading, as you choose the routes through the material depending on the needs of your group.

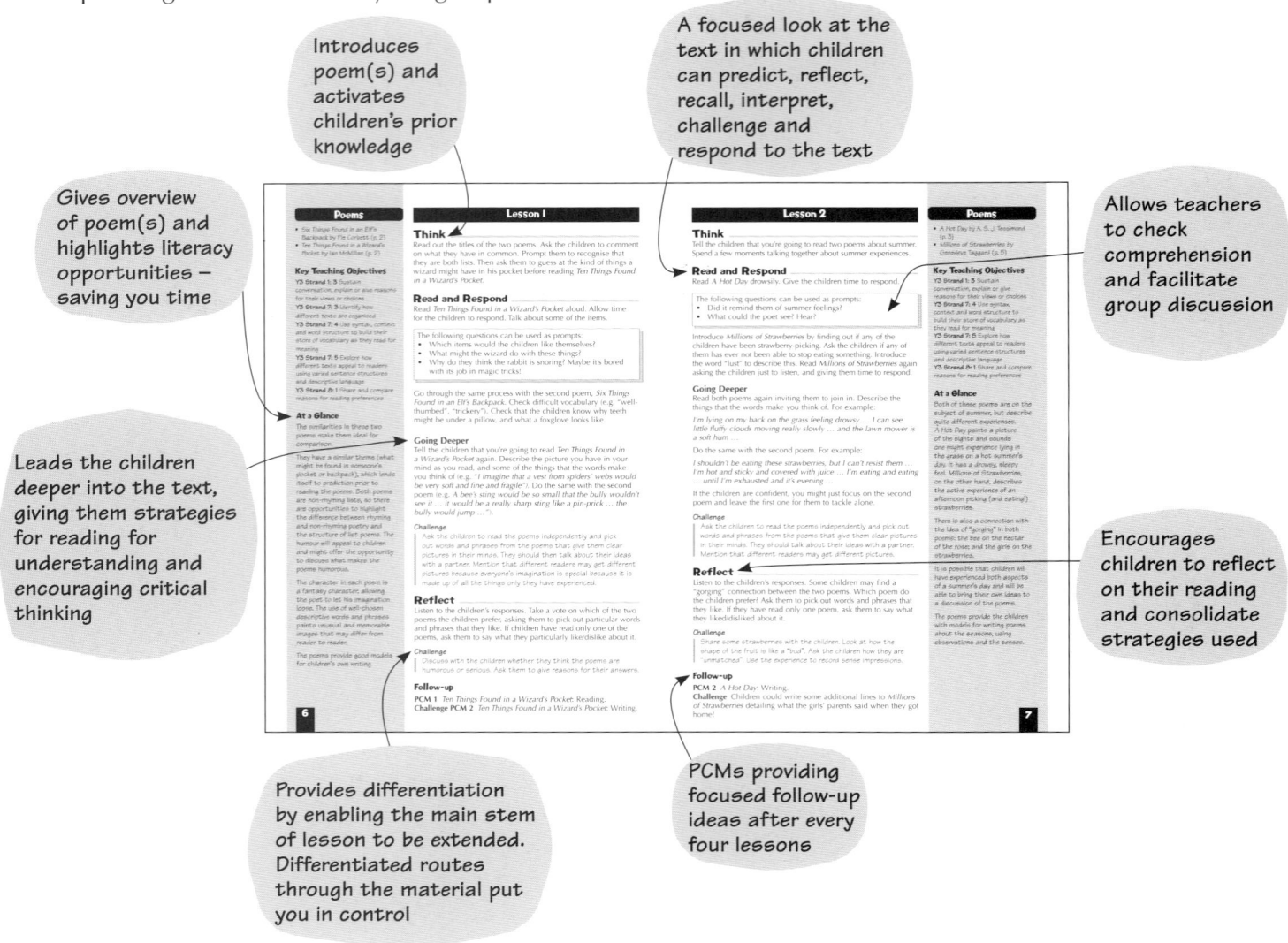

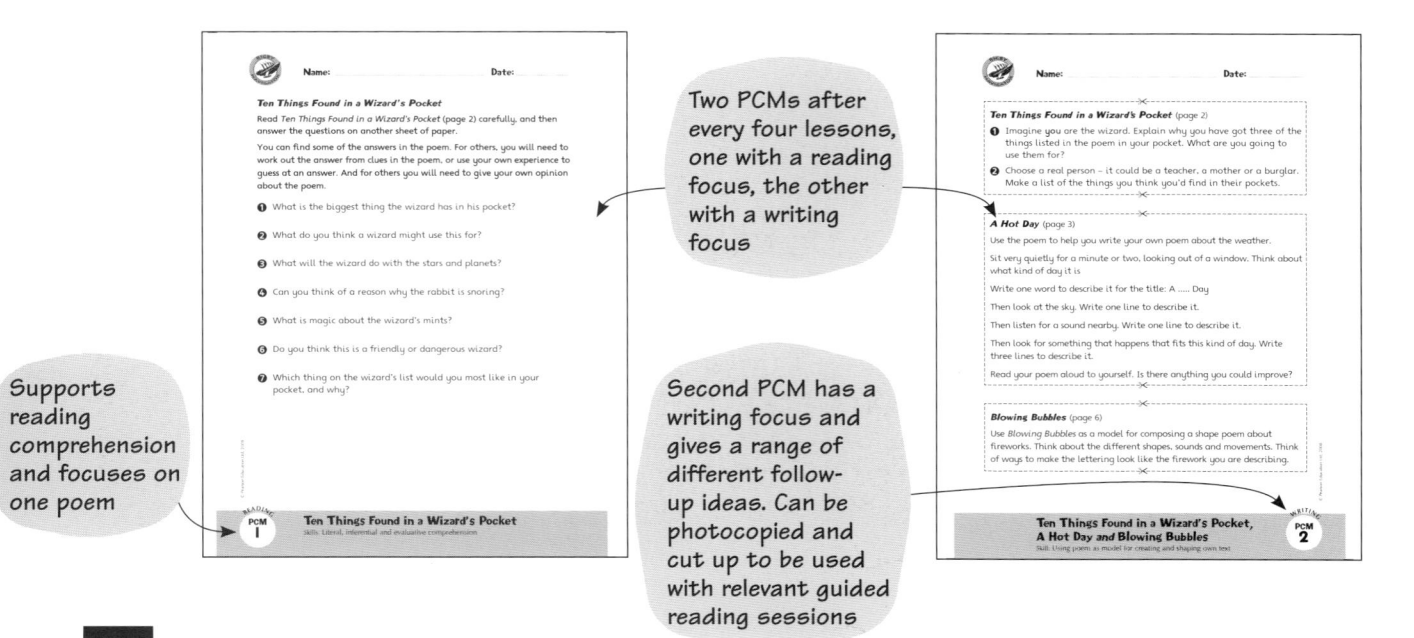

Introduces poem(s) and activates children's prior knowledge

A focused look at the text in which children can predict, reflect, recall, interpret, challenge and respond to the text

Gives overview of poem(s) and highlights literacy opportunities – saving you time

Allows teachers to check comprehension and facilitate group discussion

Leads the children deeper into the text, giving them strategies for reading for understanding and encouraging critical thinking

Encourages children to reflect on their reading and consolidate strategies used

Provides differentiation by enabling the main stem of lesson to be extended. Differentiated routes through the material put you in control

PCMs providing focused follow-up ideas after every four lessons

Two PCMs after every four lessons, one with a reading focus, the other with a writing focus

Supports reading comprehension and focuses on one poem

Second PCM has a writing focus and gives a range of different follow-up ideas. Can be photocopied and cut up to be used with relevant guided reading sessions

Renewed Framework Teaching Objectives

The Snake's Pyjamas

Lesson	Poems	Objectives	Poem type	Renewed Framework Unit
1	• *Six Things Found in an Elf's Backpack* by Pie Corbett (p. 2) • *Ten Things Found in a Wizard's Pocket* by Ian McMillan (p. 2)	**Y3 Strand 1: 3** Sustain conversation, explain or give reasons for their views or choices **Y3 Strand 7: 3** Identify how different texts are organised **Y3 Strand 7: 4** Use syntax, context and word structure to build their store of vocabulary as they read for meaning **Y3 Strand 7: 5** Explore how different texts appeal to readers using varied sentence structures and descriptive language **Y3 Strand 8: 1** Share and compare reasons for reading preferences	List poems based on observation and the senses	
2	• *A Hot Day* by A. S. J. Tessimond (p. 3) • *Millions of Strawberries* by Genevieve Taggard (p. 5)	**Y3 Strand 1: 3** Sustain conversation, explain or give reasons for their views or choices **Y3 Strand 7: 4** Use syntax, context and word structure to build their store of vocabulary as they read for meaning **Y3 Strand 7: 5** Explore how different texts appeal to readers using varied sentence structures and descriptive language **Y3 Strand 8: 1** Share and compare reasons for reading preferences	Poems based on observation and the senses	
3	• *The Caterpillar* by Christina Rossetti (p. 3) • *The Cabbage White Butterfly* by Elizabeth Jennings (p. 4)	**Y3 Strand 1: 3** Sustain conversation, explain or give reasons for their views or choices **Y3 Strand 7: 2** Infer characters' feelings **Y3 Strand 7: 3** Identify how different texts are organised **Y3 Strand 7: 5** Explore how different texts appeal to readers using varied sentence structures and descriptive language **Y3 Strand 8: 1** Share and compare reasons for reading preferences **Y3 Strand 8: 2** Empathise with characters	Poems based on observation and the senses	
4	• *Blowing Bubbles* by Patricia Leighton (p. 6) • *Listen* by Maggie Holmes (p. 7) • *Dive and Dip* by Max Fatchen (p. 8)	**Y3 Strand 1: 3** Sustain conversation, explain or give reasons for their views or choices **Y3 Strand 7: 3** Identify how different texts are organised **Y3 Strand 7: 5** Explore how different texts appeal to readers using varied sentence structures and descriptive language **Y3 Strand 8: 1** Share and compare reasons for reading preferences **Y3 Strand 8: 3** Identify features that writers use to provoke readers' reactions	Shape poems	Unit 2

5	• *Louder!* By Roger Stevens (p. 10) • *Surrounded by Noise!* by Ian Souter (p. 11)	**Y3 Strand 1: 1** Prepare poems for performance, identifying appropriate expression, tone, volume and use of voices and other sounds **Y3 Strand 1: 3** Sustain conversation, explain or give reasons for their views or choices **Y3 Strand 4: 3** Identify and discuss qualities of others' performances **Y3 Strand 7: 3** Identify how different texts are organised **Y3 Strand 7: 5** Explore how different texts appeal to readers using varied sentence structures and descriptive language **Y3 Strand 8: 3** Identify features that writers use to provoke readers' reactions	Poems to perform	Unit 1
6	• *Weather* by Eve Merriam (p. 12) • *Sea Timeless Song* by Grace Nichols (p. 13)	**Y3 Strand 1: 1** Prepare poems for performance, identifying appropriate expression, tone, volume and use of voices and other sounds **Y3 Strand 1: 3** Sustain conversation, explain or give reasons for their views or choices **Y3 Strand 4: 3** Identify and discuss qualities of others' performances **Y3 Strand 7: 3** Identify how different texts are organised **Y3 Strand 7: 5** Explore how different texts appeal to readers using varied sentence structures and descriptive language **Y3 Strand 8: 3** Identify features that writers use to provoke readers' reactions	Poems to perform	Unit 1
7	• *The Cheer-up Song* by John Whitworth (p. 14) • *A Crispy Tale* by Judith Nicholls (p. 15)	**Y3 Strand 1: 1** Prepare poems for performance, identifying appropriate expression, tone, volume and use of voices and other sounds **Y3 Strand 1: 3** Sustain conversation, explain or give reasons for their views or choices **Y3 Strand 4: 3** Identify and discuss qualities of others' performances **Y3 Strand 7: 3** Identify how different texts are organised **Y3 Strand 7: 5** Explore how different texts appeal to readers using varied sentence structures and descriptive language **Y3 Strand 8: 3** Identify features that writers use to provoke readers' reactions	Poems to perform	Unit 1
8	• Review of performance poems	**Y3 Strand 1: 1** Prepare poems for performance, identifying appropriate expression, tone, volume and use of voices and other sounds **Y3 Strand 1: 3** Sustain conversation, explain or give reasons for their views or choices **Y3 Strand 4: 3** Identify and discuss qualities of others' performances **Y3 Strand 8: 3** Identify features that writers use to provoke readers' reactions	Poems to perform	Unit 1

9	• *How Can I?* by Brian Moses (p. 16) • *Jellyfish Stew* by Jack Prelutsky (p. 18)	**Y3 Strand 1: 3** Sustain conversation, explain or give reasons for their views or choices **Y3 Strand 7: 5** Explore how different texts appeal to readers using varied sentence structures and descriptive language **Y3 Strand 8: 1** Share and compare reasons for reading preferences **Y3 Strand 8: 3** Identify features that writers use to provoke readers' reactions	Language play	Unit 3
10	• *Animal Riddle* by Pie Corbett (p. 17) • *How Did He Escape?* by Pie Corbett (p. 20)	**Y3 Strand 1: 3** Sustain conversation, explain or give reasons for their views or choices **Y3 Strand 7: 3** Identify how different texts are organised **Y3 Strand 7: 5** Explore how different texts appeal to readers using varied sentence structures and descriptive language **Y3 Strand 8: 1** Share and compare reasons for reading preferences **Y3 Strand 8: 3** Identify features that writers use to provoke readers' reactions	Language play	Unit 3
11	• *Some Favourite Words* by Richard Edwards (p. 19) • *Who Says a Poem Always Has to Rhyme?* by Roger Stevens (p. 22)	**Y3 Strand 1: 3** Sustain conversation, explain or give reasons for their views or choices **Y3 Strand 1: 4** Develop vocabulary **Y3 Strand 7: 3** Identify how different texts are organised **Y3 Strand 7: 5** Explore how different texts appeal to readers using varied sentence structures and descriptive language **Y3 Strand 8: 1** Share and compare reasons for reading preferences **Y3 Strand 8: 3** Identify features that writers use to provoke readers' reactions	Language play	Unit 3
12	• Playground rhymes (p. 23)	**Y3 Strand 1: 3** Sustain conversation, explain or give reasons for their views or choices **Y3 Strand 7: 3** Identify how different texts are organised **Y3 Strand 7: 5** Explore how different texts appeal to readers using varied sentence structures and descriptive language **Y3 Strand 8: 1** Share and compare reasons for reading preferences **Y3 Strand 8: 3** Identify features that writers use to provoke readers' reactions	Language play	Unit 3

NOTE: The strand numbers identified in the Objectives column above refer to the Renewed Framework core learning strands. They are: **Strand 1:** Speaking; **Strand 4:** Drama; **Strand 7:** Understanding and interpreting texts; **Strand 8:** Engaging with and responding to texts.

Poems

- *Six Things Found in an Elf's Backpack* by Pie Corbett (p. 2)
- *Ten Things Found in a Wizard's Pocket* by Ian McMillan (p. 2)

Key Teaching Objectives

Y3 Strand 1: 3 Sustain conversation, explain or give reasons for their views or choices

Y3 Strand 7: 3 Identify how different texts are organised

Y3 Strand 7: 4 Use syntax, context and word structure to build their store of vocabulary as they read for meaning

Y3 Strand 7: 5 Explore how different texts appeal to readers using varied sentence structures and descriptive language

Y3 Strand 8: 1 Share and compare reasons for reading preferences

At a Glance

The similarities in these two poems make them ideal for comparison.

They have a similar theme (what might be found in someone's pocket or backpack), which lends itself to prediction prior to reading the poems. Both poems are non-rhyming lists, so there are opportunities to highlight the difference between rhyming and non-rhyming poetry and the structure of list poems. The humour will appeal to children and might offer the opportunity to discuss what makes the poems humorous.

The character in each poem is a fantasy character, allowing the poet to let his imagination loose. The use of well-chosen descriptive words and phrases paints unusual and memorable images that may differ from reader to reader.

The poems provide good models for children's own writing.

Lesson 1

Think

Read out the titles of the two poems. Ask the children to comment on what they have in common. Prompt them to recognise that they are both lists. Then ask them to guess at the kind of things a wizard might have in his pocket before reading *Ten Things Found in a Wizard's Pocket*.

Read and Respond

Read *Ten Things Found in a Wizard's Pocket* aloud. Allow time for the children to respond. Talk about some of the items.

> The following questions can be used as prompts:
> - Which items would the children like themselves?
> - What might the wizard do with these things?
> - Why do they think the rabbit is snoring? Maybe it's bored with its job in magic tricks!

Go through the same process with the second poem, *Six Things Found in an Elf's Backpack*. Check difficult vocabulary (e.g. "well-thumbed", "trickery"). Check that the children know why teeth might be under a pillow, and what a foxglove looks like.

Going Deeper

Tell the children that you're going to read *Ten Things Found in a Wizard's Pocket* again. Describe the picture you have in your mind as you read, and some of the things that the words make you think of (e.g. *"I imagine that a vest from spiders' webs would be very soft and fine and fragile"*). Do the same with the second poem (e.g. *A bee's sting would be so small that the bully wouldn't see it … it would be a really sharp sting like a pin-prick … the bully would jump …"*).

Challenge

Ask the children to read the poems independently and pick out words and phrases from the poems that give them clear pictures in their minds. They should then talk about their ideas with a partner. Mention that different readers may get different pictures because everyone's imagination is special because it is made up of all the things only they have experienced.

Reflect

Listen to the children's responses. Take a vote on which of the two poems the children prefer, asking them to pick out particular words and phrases that they like. If children have read only one of the poems, ask them to say what they particularly like/dislike about it.

Challenge

Discuss with the children whether they think the poems are humorous or serious. Ask them to give reasons for their answers.

Follow-up

PCM 1 *Ten Things Found in a Wizard's Pocket*: Reading.
Challenge PCM 2 *Ten Things Found in a Wizard's Pocket*: Writing.

Lesson 2

Think
Tell the children that you're going to read two poems about summer. Spend a few moments talking together about summer experiences.

Read and Respond
Read *A Hot Day* drowsily. Give the children time to respond.

> The following questions can be used as prompts:
> - Did it remind them of summer feelings?
> - What could the poet see? Hear?

Introduce *Millions of Strawberries* by finding out if any of the children have been strawberry-picking. Ask the children if any of them has ever not been able to stop eating something. Introduce the word "lust" to describe this. Read *Millions of Strawberries* asking the children just to listen, and giving them time to respond.

Going Deeper
Read both poems again inviting them to join in. Describe the things that the words make you think of. For example:

I'm lying on my back on the grass feeling drowsy ... I can see little fluffy clouds moving really slowly ... and the lawn mower is a soft hum ...

Do the same with the second poem. For example:

I shouldn't be eating these strawberries, but I can't resist them ... I'm hot and sticky and covered with juice ... I'm eating and eating ... until I'm exhausted and it's evening ...

If the children are confident, you might just focus on the second poem and leave the first one for them to tackle alone.

Challenge
Ask the children to read the poems independently and pick out words and phrases from the poems that give them clear pictures in their minds. They should talk about their ideas with a partner. Mention that different readers may get different pictures.

Reflect
Listen to the children's responses. Some children may find a "gorging" connection between the two poems. Which poem do the children prefer? Ask them to pick out words and phrases that they like. If they have read only one poem, ask them to say what they liked/disliked about it.

Challenge
Share some strawberries with the children. Look at how the shape of the fruit is like a "bud". Ask the children how they are "unmatched". Use the experience to record sense impressions.

Follow-up
PCM 2 *A Hot Day*: Writing.
Challenge Children could write some additional lines to *Millions of Strawberries* detailing what the girls' parents said when they got home!

Poems
- *A Hot Day* by A. S. J. Tessimond (p. 3)
- *Millions of Strawberries* by Genevieve Taggard (p. 5)

Key Teaching Objectives
Y3 Strand 1: 3 Sustain conversation, explain or give reasons for their views or choices
Y3 Strand 7: 4 Use syntax, context and word structure to build their store of vocabulary as they read for meaning
Y3 Strand 7: 5 Explore how different texts appeal to readers using varied sentence structures and descriptive language
Y3 Strand 8: 1 Share and compare reasons for reading preferences

At a Glance
Both of these poems are on the subject of summer, but describe quite different experiences. *A Hot Day* paints a picture of the sights and sounds one might experience lying in the grass on a hot summer's day. It has a drowsy, sleepy feel. *Millions of Strawberries*, on the other hand, describes the active experience of an afternoon picking (and eating!) strawberries.

There is also a connection with the idea of "gorging" in both poems: the bee on the nectar of the rose; and the girls on the strawberries.

It is possible that children will have experienced both aspects of a summer's day and will be able to bring their own ideas to a discussion of the poems.

The poems provide the children with models for writing poems about the seasons, using observations and the senses.

Poems

- *The Caterpillar* by Christina Rossetti (p. 3)
- *The Cabbage White Butterfly* by Elizabeth Jennings (p. 4)

Key Teaching Objectives

Y3 Strand 1: 3 Sustain conversation, explain or give reasons for their views or choices
Y3 Strand 7: 2 Infer characters' feelings
Y3 Strand 7: 3 Identify how different texts are organised
Y3 Strand 7: 5 Explore how different texts appeal to readers using varied sentence structures and descriptive language
Y3 Strand 8: 1 Share and compare reasons for reading preferences
Y3 Strand 8: 2 Empathise with characters

At a Glance

These poems are ideal for reading together as they each focus on a different creature in the life cycle of a butterfly – i.e. the caterpillar and the butterfly.

Children may be interested to learn that *The Caterpillar* was written over 150 years ago – caterpillars were just the same then!

Each poem is written in a different voice. In *The Caterpillar* the poet is talking to the caterpillar; in *The Cabbage White Butterfly* it is the butterfly who is speaking to the reader.

The descriptive words and phrases will give children the opportunity to explore how the poets create images, and to discuss how these images may differ from reader to reader.

Both poems raise the issue of 'enemies' and *The Cabbage White Butterfly*, in particular, points to humans as the enemy, eliciting empathy from readers.

These are rhyming poems and, if appropriate for your children, you may wish to look at the rhyme patterns.

Lesson 3

Think

Ask the children what caterpillars and butterflies have in common. Ensure they understand the life cycle of a butterfly.

Read and Respond

Read *The Caterpillar* aloud to the children and allow time for them to respond.

> The following questions can be used as prompts:
> - Who is the poet speaking to in this poem? *The caterpillar.*
> - What words or phrases does the poet use to describe the caterpillar? *Brown, furry, in a hurry.*
> - What does the phrase "Spin and die" mean? *It refers to the part of the life cycle where the caterpillar spins a cocoon and dies as a caterpillar before it becomes a butterfly.*

Go through the same process with *The Cabbage White Butterfly*.

> The following questions can be used as prompts:
> - Who is speaking in this poem? *The butterfly.*
> - What words or phrases does the poet use to describe the butterfly's fragility? *Like a flower, delicate wings, silent.*

Going Deeper

Read *The Caterpillar* again inviting them to join in. Describe the things that the words make you think of (e.g. *I can see the hairy caterpillar looping along a twig looking for somewhere to hide and make its cocoon*). Now ask them to do the same with *The Cabbage White Butterfly* and to discuss their ideas with a partner. Remind them that different readers may get different pictures because everyone's imagination is unique.

Challenge

> Discuss the things that the poems have in common. As well as both being about creatures in the same life cycle, both the creatures are hiding from their enemies. Who are the enemies in each case? In The Caterpillar the enemies are a toad and bird; in The Cabbage White Butterfly the enemy is human beings.

Reflect

Listen to the children's responses. Take a vote on which of the two poems the children prefer, asking them to read out words and phrases that they like. If children have read only one poem, ask them what they liked/disliked about it.

Challenge

> Discuss with the children why the butterfly (in *The Cabbage White Butterfly*) thought a cloud had come down, and what they think the last line means.

Follow-up

No PCM The children could identify the rhyming words and rhyme pattern in each poem.
Challenge The children could work in pairs to write 'companion' poems about a tadpole and a frog.

Lesson 4

Think
Introduce the idea of writing poems in shapes that fit the subject of the poem. Some children may already be familiar with shape poems and can talk about ones they have read. Read *Blowing Bubbles* to the children without letting them look at the poem. Tell them it is a shape poem. Ask them to imagine, as you read, what it might look like. Were their images anything like the poet's?

Read and Respond
Read *Blowing Bubbles* again, with the children joining in.

> The following questions can be used as prompts:
> - What do the different shapes represent? *The letters on their sides show the bubbles turning round; the jagged edges show the bubbles bursting; the letters jumping up show the bubbles touching a surface, and bouncing up before bursting.*
> - What does the layout add to the poem? *It provides an image that supports the text and adds more meaning than the words alone give.*

Going Deeper
Tell the children they are going to look carefully at the layout of another poem. Read *Listen* aloud, and then again with the children joining in.
- How does the poet show the raindrops and water ripples? *The words are set vertically to show the raindrops and in wavy lines to show the ripples.*
- Why do the words get more wobbly? *To show the increasingly violent movement of the water in the sea.*
- Can you identify some rhymes?

Challenge
Ask the children to read *Dive and Dip* independently. Discuss how the shape echoes the subject matter; the up and down movement of a roller coaster. Ask them to identify the rhymes within lines as well as those at the end of each couplet. They may pick up on the way the –ing endings convey movement.

Reflect
As well as the shape of each poem, what other poetic devices can the children identify? *For example in* Blowing Bubbles, *rhyme, comparisons (Bubbles are rainbows), repetition (float), alliteration (bubbles are beautiful).*

Challenge
Ask those who read more than one poem which they prefer. They should select words or phrases to justify their preference.

Follow-up
PCM 2 *Blowing Bubbles*: Writing.
Challenge Challenge a partner to write a shape poem on a given subject.

Poems
- *Blowing Bubbles* by Patricia Leighton (p. 6)
- *Listen* by Maggie Holmes (p. 7)
- *Dive and Dip* by Max Fatchen (p. 8)

Key Teaching Objectives
Y3 Strand 1: 3 Sustain conversation, explain or give reasons for their views or choices
Y3 Strand 7: 3 Identify how different texts are organised
Y3 Strand 7: 5 Explore how different texts appeal to readers using varied sentence structures and descriptive language
Y3 Strand 8: 1 Share and compare reasons for reading preferences
Y3 Strand 8: 3 Identify features that writers use to provoke readers' reactions

At a Glance
Shape poems mix visual and verbal images, so that they are half picture and half poem. A shape poem takes the shape of its subject matter.

These three poems provide a variety of visually exciting examples of shape poems, giving opportunities for children to discuss how layout contributes to meaning.

As well as using shape, the poets also use other poetic devices such as rhyme, comparison imagery, repetition and alliteration – all of which children can be asked to identify.

The three different poems provide an opportunity for children to share and compare their preferences, referring back to the texts to support their choices.

Name: _____ **Date:** _____

Ten Things Found in a Wizard's Pocket

Read *Ten Things Found in a Wizard's Pocket* (page 2) carefully, and then answer the questions on another sheet of paper.

You can find some of the answers in the poem. For others, you will need to work out the answer from clues in the poem, or use your own experience to guess at an answer. And for others you will need to give your own opinion about the poem.

❶ What is the biggest thing the wizard has in his pocket?

❷ What do you think a wizard might use this for?

❸ What will the wizard do with the stars and planets?

❹ Can you think of a reason why the rabbit is snoring?

❺ What is magic about the wizard's mints?

❻ Do you think this is a friendly or dangerous wizard?

❼ Which thing on the wizard's list would you most like in your pocket, and why?

Ten Things Found in a Wizard's Pocket
Skills: Literal, inferential and evaluative comprehension

Name: _____   **Date:** _____

Ten Things Found in a Wizard's Pocket (page 2)

❶ Imagine **you** are the wizard. Explain why you have got three of the things listed in the poem in your pocket. What are you going to use them for?

❷ Choose a real person – it could be a teacher, a mother or a burglar. Make a list of the things you think you'd find in their pockets.

A Hot Day (page 3)

Use the poem to help you write your own poem about the weather.

Sit very quietly for a minute or two, looking out of a window. Think about what kind of day it is

Write one word to describe it for the title: A ..... Day

Then look at the sky. Write one line to describe it.

Then listen for a sound nearby. Write one line to describe it.

Then look for something that happens that fits this kind of day. Write three lines to describe it.

Read your poem aloud to yourself. Is there anything you could improve?

Blowing Bubbles (page 6)

Use *Blowing Bubbles* as a model for composing a shape poem about fireworks. Think about the different shapes, sounds and movements. Think of ways to make the lettering look like the firework you are describing.

Ten Things Found in a Wizard's Pocket, A Hot Day and Blowing Bubbles

Skill: Using poem as model for creating and shaping own text

WRITING PCM 2

Poems

- *Louder!* by Roger Stevens (p. 10)
- *Surrounded by Noise!* by Ian Souter (p. 11)

Key Teaching Objectives

Y3 Strand 1: 1 Prepare poems for performance, identifying appropriate expression, tone, volume and use of voices and other sounds

Y3 Strand 1: 3 Sustain conversation, explain or give reasons for their views or choices

Y3 Strand 4: 3 Identify and discuss qualities of others' performances

Y3 Strand 7: 3 Identify how different texts are organised

Y3 Strand 7: 5 Explore how different texts appeal to readers using varied sentence structures and descriptive language

Y3 Strand 8: 3 Identify features that writers use to provoke readers' reactions

At a Glance

These poems were written to be performed. Both their print and layout features (varying font types and sizes, punctuation) and their subject matter (volume and noise) indicate that they are intended for performance.

As such they provide material for children to practise reading aloud with appropriate expression, tone and volume, and to be creative about how to simulate sound effects. The children will also be able to evaluate others' performances.

Children will be able to explore the structure of the poems and relate structure to meaning.

Surrounded by Noise!, with its strong verbs and onomatopoeic words, provides an excellent opportunity to discuss how the poet creates effects with word choices.

Lesson 5

Think

Explain that some poems are meant to be performed – and ensure children understand what 'performing' means – putting on a show, acting. Read the poem *Louder!* dramatically to the children before they look at it on the page. The scenario will be familiar to most children who have rehearsed for a school assembly! Ask them to identify the two speakers.

Read and Respond

Now read the poem again, with the children following and joining in, if appropriate. Discuss the features of performance poetry illustrated by this poem.

> The following questions can be used as prompts:
> - What do the children notice about the size of the print? *It gets bigger as the volume gets louder.*
> - How does the punctuation show you how to say the lines? *Commas tell you where to pause; dots indicate a trailing off of the voice; dashes indicate a sharp separation of syllables/words.*
> - What clues tell you the teacher is getting more and more exasperated? *He/she starts by saying "please", then tells Andrew he isn't trying, then the expression "for goodness sake" leads to an exasperated "LOUDER! LOUDER!" with capital letters and exclamation marks.*
> - How should Andrew's last line be read? *It should be shouted because the type size is large and the teacher then tells him not to be silly.*

Going Deeper

Read *Surrounded by Noise!* with the children joining in.
- What features of the print and layout help you to read the poem well? *Include capitalisation, exclamation marks, use of dots (ellipsis).*
- Describe some of the sounds. *Such as the rhythmic beat of the music, the vibrating whirr of a drill.*

Challenge

Ask the children to practise reading *Surrounded by Noise!* aloud in pairs. Encourage them to be inventive with sound effects.

Reflect

Ask pairs of children to read either poem aloud. Ask the rest of the group to evaluate. Then discuss anything that could be improved.

Challenge

What is it about the subject matter of these two poems that makes them really 'come to life' when they are performed rather than just read?

Follow-up

PCM 3 *Surrounded by Noise!*: Reading.
Challenge PCM 4 *Surrounded by Noise!*: Writing.

Lesson 6

Think
Ask the children to listen to the two poems as you read them aloud. Then encourage the children to comment on the 'sound' of each poem and to respond to their contrasting moods.

Read and Respond
Read *Weather* aloud again with the children joining in. Emphasise the sound of the rain as it gets stronger in each verse. Discuss the features of the poem that will help in performing it well.

> The following questions can be used as prompts:
> - Which words in the first verse give the short, sharp sound of raindrops? *For example dot, spack, speck, flick, flack, fleck.*
> - Which words are wet-sounding words? What have they got in common? *Such as slosh, galosh, slither, slather. They are words with an 's' sound.*
> - How does the lack of punctuation in many of the lines help tell you how to say them? *It indicates the line should be read quickly and continuously, without pauses, like the falling rain.*

Going Deeper
Read *Sea Timeless Song* with the children joining in. Make this as dreamy and hypnotic as you can, imitating the sounds of waves on a beach.
- What effect does the repetition of sea have? *It imitates the ongoing, repetitive sound and motion of waves and gives the poem a dreamy, hypnotic feel.*
- What effect does the use of dots (ellipsis) have? *It slows the poem down.*

Challenge
Ask the children to practise reading either poem aloud in pairs. Remind them to watch out for the patterns and punctuation, and to try to create the right mood.

Reflect
Listen to one or more pairs of children reading the poem of their choice. Ask them to evaluate their own attempt. Remind them to be positive first, and then invite them to think about improvements. The rest of the group can contribute suggestions.

Challenge
Ask the children to scan both poems to find any rhyming words. They should notice that in both the rhyme schemes are not regular but there is a lot of repetition and onomatopoeia (words that sound like their meaning). Discuss how *Weather* uses made-up words that we can understand because they imitate sounds and actions we know.

Follow-up
PCM 4 *Weather:* Writing.
Challenge Use the pattern in *Sea Timeless Song* as a model to imitate in own poem.

Poems
- *Weather* by Eve Merriam (p. 12)
- *Sea Timeless Song* by Grace Nichols (p. 13)

Key Teaching Objectives
Y3 Strand 1: 1 Prepare poems for performance, identifying appropriate expression, tone, volume and use of voices and other sounds
Y3 Strand 1: 3 Sustain conversation, explain or give reasons for their views or choices
Y3 Strand 4: 3 Identify and discuss qualities of others' performances
Y3 Strand 7: 3 Identify how different texts are organised
Y3 Strand 7: 5 Explore how different texts appeal to readers using varied sentence structures and descriptive language
Y3 Strand 8: 3 Identify features that writers use to provoke readers' reactions

At a Glance
These two poems, with their contrasting moods, lend themselves to performance.

They both provide opportunities for thinking about how sounds, meanings and repetition of words help us to perform poems well – e.g. in *Weather*, onomatopoeic words (flick, slosh) and words ending in 't' and 'k' (dot, fleck); and in *Sea Timeless Song*, the repetition of "sea timeless".

Weather also gives children the opportunity to understand the concept of 'poetic licence' and the use of 'made-up' words.

Sea Timeless Song offers an excellent, simple model for the children's own writing.

Poems

- *The Cheer-up Song* by John Whitworth (p. 14)
- *A Crispy Tale* by Judith Nicholls (p. 15)

Key Teaching Objectives

Y3 Strand 1: 1 Prepare poems for performance, identifying appropriate expression, tone, volume and use of voices and other sounds

Y3 Strand 1: 3 Sustain conversation, explain or give reasons for their views or choices

Y3 Strand 4: 3 Identify and discuss qualities of others' performances

Y3 Strand 7: 3 Identify how different texts are organised

Y3 Strand 7: 5 Explore how different texts appeal to readers using varied sentence structures and descriptive language

Y3 Strand 8: 3 Identify features that writers use to provoke readers' reactions

At a Glance

Children will relish taking on the role of the 'boaster' in *The Cheer-up Song*, and will enjoy the silliness of the cautionary tale of *A Crispy Tale*.

The Cheer-up Song offers the opportunity to look closely at how word choice and layout are chosen to appeal to readers and, in this case, to signpost how the poem should be read aloud. The poem presents challenges with some unusual vocabulary and a tricky rhythm.

A Crispy Tale is not broken up into verses and not every line begins with a capital letter. This gives children the opportunity to explore how structure is a signpost to how the poem should be read aloud.

Both poems, when performed, offer children the opportunity to evaluate their own, and others', performances.

Lesson 7

Think

Tell the children that the two poems in this lesson are suitable for performing out loud. Discuss what kind of features they might expect (such as catchy rhythms, funny rhymes, interesting sounds, unusual fonts and type sizes). Then read *The Cheer-up Song*.

Read and Respond

Read the poem again inviting the children to join in. Clap the rhythm to help them. Check their understanding of the poem.

> The following questions can be used as prompts:
> - Why do you think the poem is called *The Cheer-up Song*? *The poet is trying to cheer himself up by listing all the ways in which he is great!*
> - What is the meaning of the word "patella"? *Knee cap.* What does the poet mean by "bumble-bee's patella". *The bee's knees, an expression meaning 'the best'.*
> - Why are some of the words hyphenated? *To slow down the saying of the words in order to emphasise their meaning.*

Going Deeper

Read *A Crispy Tale* with the children joining in. Discuss the features that give clues as to how the poem should be read aloud.
- What is unusual about the layout? *No separate verses. Capital letters only used at the start of lines that begin a new sentence. These indicate that the poem should be read like a story.*
- What do the dots (ellipsis) and dash tell you? *To pause at the end of the lines on which they occur.*
- How should the word "CRISP!" be said? *The capital letters and exclamation mark indicate that it should be said loudly.*
- How should the words "Crunch!" and "guzzle" be said? *These words sound like their meaning, so they should be said like the sound they represent.* (Introduce onomatopoeia if appropriate.)

Challenge
Ask the children to practise reading either poem aloud in pairs. Remind them to look out for the patterns and punctuation.

Reflect

Listen to pairs of children read their chosen poem. Ask them to evaluate their own attempt. Ask the rest of the group for an evaluation.

Challenge
Ask the children to say which of the poems they prefer and to give reasons for their choice.

Follow-up

PCM 2 *The Cheer-up Song*: Writing.
Challenge Think of a different title for *A Crispy Tale*.

Lesson 8

Think

Recap on some of the features of performance poetry (for example catchy rhythms, interesting sounds, funny rhymes, unusual structures). Remind the children that when they are reading a performance poem, the punctuation and other layout details will help them to read the poem well.

Read and Respond

Ask the children, working in pairs or larger groups, to browse through the performance poems in *The Snake's Pyjamas* anthology that they haven't explored in detail yet. They should then choose one and plan how they are going to perform it.

> The following questions can be used as prompts:
> - Does the poem have a regular or unusual rhythm? (Clapping the poem as they read will help.)
> - Does the layout give you any clues as to how the poem should be performed?
> - What punctuation is there to help you?
> - Are there any words in a different font or size?

Going Deeper

Rather than performing the poem in chorus, ask the children to allocate parts or lines to different children and to use the different voices to give added 'texture' to the performance.

Challenge

Ask the children to discuss (and implement if appropriate) extended performance ideas, such as adding sound effects and/or musical accompaniment.

Reflect

Listen to some of the performances. Take a vote on a group favourite poem, and finish the session with a performance of it.

Challenge

Put together a performance of all the poems for a wider audience, perhaps for an assembly or for parents.

Follow-up

No PCM The children could copy out a verse or section of one of the poems and annotate it with notes on how to perform it.
Challenge The children could exchange their annotated 'scripts' with a partner and read aloud according to each other's directions.

Poems

Review of all performance poems

Key Teaching Objectives

Y3 Strand 1: 1 Prepare poems for performance, identifying appropriate expression, tone, volume and use of voices and other sounds
Y3 Strand 1: 3 Sustain conversation, explain or give reasons for their views or choices
Y3 Strand 4: 3 Identify and discuss qualities of others' performances
Y3 Strand 8: 3 Identify features that writers use to provoke readers' reactions

At a Glance

The purpose of this lesson is to review all the performance poems and to reinforce reading with expression.

The children should be given time to browse through the relevant section of *The Snake's Pyjamas* (pages 10–15) and to choose one of the poems they haven't read before (or their favourite one if they've read them all) for a polished performance.

Providing children with a wider audience than their guided reading group will provide added motivation.

Name: _____ **Date:** _____

Surrounded by Noise!

Read *Surrounded by Noise!* (page 11) carefully, and then answer the questions on another sheet of paper.

You can find some of the answers in the poem. For others, you will need to work out the answer from clues in the poem, or use your own experience to guess at an answer. And for others you will need to give your own opinion about the poem.

1. Find four things that make a noise in the poem.

2. What is the workman doing? How do you know?

3. What clue tells you that Mum doesn't like noise?

4. Why do you think that some words are in capital letters?

5. What noise does the poet hear when the plane climbs the sky?

6. Can you think of other words to describe the sound of cars or trains?

7. What do you think the poet wants us to think about when we read the poem?

8. Do you think the noises in the town are worse than in the countryside? Explain why you think this.

© Pearson Education Ltd, 2008

PCM 3

Surrounded by Noise!
Skills: Literal, inferential and evaluative comprehension

Name: _____ **Date:** _____

Surrounded by Noise! (page 11)

Sit and listen to the sounds that surround you. Maybe they are quite different from the sounds in the poem. Perhaps you live in the country. Think of or make up words to describe the sounds. Then write your own poem. You could use the same pattern as *Surrounded by Noise!*

Weather (page 12)

❶ Practise reading the poem aloud with sound effects. Choose percussion instruments that fit the words. For example, a wood block could make a "*dot dot*" sound.

❷ What other weather poems can you find? Browse through some anthologies and make your own collection. Maybe you could add some weather paintings or collages.

The Cheer-up Song (page 14)

It's fun to boast sometimes! Have a go at thinking of some wonderful compliments about yourself. They can be as crazy as you like. Try and make your poem rhyme in the same way as *The Cheer-up Song*.

Here's one to start you off:
I'm the king of the castle
I'm the icing on the cake
I'm …

Surrounded by Noise!, Weather and The Cheer-up Song

Skill: Using poem as model for creating and shaping own text

PCM 4

WRITING

Poems

- *How Can I?* by Brian Moses (p. 16)
- *Jellyfish Stew* by Jack Prelutsky (p. 18)

Key Teaching Objectives

Y3 Strand 1: 3 Sustain conversation, explain or give reasons for their views or choices
Y3 Strand 7: 5 Explore how different texts appeal to readers using varied sentence structures and descriptive language
Y3 Strand 8: 1 Share and compare reasons for reading preferences
Y3 Strand 8: 3 Identify features that writers use to provoke readers' reactions

At a Glance

These humorous poems are fine examples of poetry that uses language play.

In *Jellyfish Stew* the poet describes, in an 'over-the-top' way, how much he loves this made-up food item. It is full of words and phrases that taste good on the tongue and provides opportunities to discuss such poetic devices as rhyme, alliteration and onomatopoeia.

How Can I? is funny in a different way. It is based on the joke of using common, everyday expressions in a literal way. It gives children the opportunity to explore these expressions and to observe how a poet can take language and manipulate it to create new meaning.

The two poems are ideal for learning by heart, a skill that directs children's attention to the details of structure and meaning in the poem.

Lesson 9

Think

Read out the title of the poem *Jellyfish Stew*. Ask the children what type of poem they think this might be. Steer them towards identifying it as a nonsense or humorous poem. Then read the poem with as much relish as possible. Were they right?

Read and Respond

Read *Jellyfish Stew* a second time inviting the children to join in, and keeping up a swinging rhythm. Allow time for the children to respond.

> The following questions can be used as prompts:
> - How can you tell this is a humorous poem? *It is about a silly, made-up subject (jellyfish stew). The stew is clearly revolting but, nonetheless, the poet loves it!*
> - Read the first line several times in succession. What do you notice about it? *It is a bit of tongue twister and fun to say.*
> - What other words or phrases do you particularly like? *For example loony, creepy, revolting, smelly, bog down my belly, oozy spoonful.*
> - Can you find examples of alliteration (words that are next to or near each other that begin with the same letter)? *Such as soggy/smelly/shampoo; bog/belly.*
> - Can you find examples of onomatopoeia (words that sound like their meaning)? *For example hullabaloo, oodles of goo.*

Going Deeper

Explain that the next poem you're going to read is funny in a different way. Read *How Can I?* aloud to the children, and then again with them joining in. Why is this poem funny? *It takes common everyday expressions and uses them literally.*

What are some of these expressions and what do they really mean? *For example "wind up" means to annoy/aggravate; "turn on" means to display/show.*

Challenge

Brainstorm similar expressions (such as stiff upper lip, hold your tongue, drives you round the bend, etc.).

Reflect

Listen to the children's responses. Ask them to describe how each of the poems (or the one they read) 'play(s) with words'. Encourage them to pick out particular words and phrases they like.

Challenge

Ask the children to choose one of the two poems to learn by heart. Give them some tips for learning by heart (such as add one more line each time until you can say it all, chant it over and over with a partner, ask a partner to prompt you, etc.).

Follow-up

PCM 5 *Jellyfish Stew*: Reading.
Challenge PCM 6 *How Can I?*: Writing.

Lesson 10

Think
Introduce the two poems by explaining that they are both riddles and are written by the same poet, Pie Corbett. Can they remember another poem by Pie Corbett that they have read in this book? (*Six Things Found in an Elf's Backpack,* page 2).

Read and Respond
Explain to the children that the first poem you are going to read is an 'acrostic' poem, but don't yet explain what acrostic means. Ask the children to look at the text of *Animal riddle* as you read it aloud. Then discuss their responses to it.

> The following questions can be used as prompts:
> - What do you notice about the format of the poem? *They should have spotted the seemingly incidental capital letters.*
> - What do these capital letters mean? *Reading down they spell "badger" which is the answer to the riddle.*
> - Explain that this poem is in the form of an acrostic puzzle. What do they think that means? *An acrostic puzzle is one in which certain letters form a word when read vertically.*
> - How do you think the poet set about writing the poem? *Maybe he wrote the word down the page first and then built the lines around the main letters.*

Going Deeper
Read the second riddle poem *How Did He Escape?* just to the end of the first page (up to "*how was it done?*"). Ask the children to predict answers to this question. Then read the second part of the poem; the answer. Leave a moment for it to sink in!
- What is funny about the answer to the riddle? *The poet has used words that sound the same but have different meanings and spellings (homophones).*
- What homophones has he used? *Sore/saw; whole/hole; hoarse/horse.*

Challenge
Spend a few moments looking more closely at the riddle itself (page 20). Ask the children to find its rhymes. Is there a pattern? They should also notice the uneven line length and the occasional internal rhyme (such as rot/jot).

Reflect
Sum up the main difference between the two poems (*namely that* Animal riddle *is based on a visual joke while* How Did He Escape? *is based on an aural one*). Take a vote on the favourite and discuss reasons for preferences.

Challenge
Children could learn the 'answer' to *How Did He Escape?* by heart.

Follow-up
PCM 6 *Animal riddle*: Writing.
Challenge Ask children to find other words that are homophones in the answer part of *How Did He Escape?*

Poems
- *Animal Riddle* by Pie Corbett (p. 17)
- *How Did He Escape?* by Pie Corbett (p. 20)

Key Teaching Objectives
Y3 Strand 1: 3 Sustain conversation, explain or give reasons for their views or choices
Y3 Strand 7: 3 Identify how different texts are organised
Y3 Strand 7: 5 Explore how different texts appeal to readers using varied sentence structures and descriptive language
Y3 Strand 8: 1 Share and compare reasons for reading preferences
Y3 Strand 8: 3 Identify features that writers use to provoke readers' reactions

At a Glance
These poems are riddles with integrated answers. They both use language play, but in different ways.

Animal riddle is a non-rhyming poem that plays with language in a visual way. It is an acrostic poem in which the answer to the riddle can be found by reading vertically the capital letters placed within some of the lines. It also has elements of kenning in it (for example barrel rider, midnight feaster, zebra bear).

How Did He Escape? plays with language in an aural way. The answer to the riddle (and the question in the title) is based on playing with homophones.

The poems provide opportunities for exploring how poems are structured – for example, whether they are rhyming or non-rhyming and if the latter, whether there is an identifiable pattern.

As the two poems are by the same poet, children have the opportunity to compare and contrast the poet's work.

Poems

- *Some Favourite Words* by Richard Edwards (p. 19)
- *Who Says a Poem Always Has to Rhyme?* by Roger Stevens (p. 22)

Key Teaching Objectives

Y3 Strand 1: 3 Sustain conversation, explain or give reasons for their views or choices

Y3 Strand 1: 4 Develop vocabulary

Y3 Strand 7: 3 Identify how different texts are organised

Y3 Strand 7: 5 Explore how different texts appeal to readers using varied sentence structures and descriptive language

Y3 Strand 8: 1 Share and compare reasons for reading preferences

Y3 Strand 8: 3 Identify features that writers use to provoke readers' reactions

At a Glance

These poems offer children opportunities to further explore forms of humour and language play in poetry.

Some Favourite Words has similarities to a list poem – it's a list of the poet's favourite words – although it is written in verse form. It will give children the opportunity to think about the sound of words and to discuss words that they like, and why. The words are wonderfully diverse with onomatopoeic qualities and offer opportunities for children to develop their vocabulary.

Some Favourite Words has an easily recognisable rhyme pattern (ababb), and therefore offers opportunities for comparison with *Who Says a Poem Always Has to Rhyme?*

Who Says a Poem Always Has to Rhyme? offers a challenge in reading as its format is unusual (it uses asterisks and footnotes). The joke of the poem is that it is both rhyming (implicit) and non-rhyming (explicit)!

Lesson 11

Think

Talk about enjoying the sound of words, even if you don't know what they mean. Refer back to words in poems already read, for example *hullabaloo, clackety, puddmuddle*. Give a personal example of a word you like saying and ask individual children to offer some of their own.

Read and Respond

Read aloud *Some Favourite Words*, emphasising the sounds in each word. Read it again with the children joining in. Discuss their responses.

> The following questions can be used as prompts:
> - Which words stood out in particular for you? Explain why.
> - Are there any words in the poem that make you laugh? *For example bamboozle, dumbledore.*
> - Can you guess their meanings? *For example bamboozle – to cheat or mystify; dumbledore – a bumblebee (and a character in* Harry Potter!*).*
> - Which words sound like their meaning (remind them of the term *onomatopoeia*)? *Could include whoop, ooze.*
> - Is this a rhyming poem? *Yes.* Can you see a rhyme pattern? *ababb.*

Going Deeper

Ask the children to look at the poem *Who Says a Poem Always Has to Rhyme?* See if they can work out for themselves how to read it. Let them read it as a group or in pairs.
- What do the asterisks mean? (Explain the idea of footnotes, if they don't already know.) *They refer the reader to the text at the bottom of the page.*
- How is this poet "playing with language"? *He has deliberately left out the rhyming word at the end of each couplet, and provided non-rhyming alternatives as footnotes.*
- What are the rhymes you might expect? *Bank, cola, socks, rhyme.*
- Why are the alternatives funny? *They are a surprise, particularly the far-too-long last line.*

Challenge

Ask the children to work in pairs to prepare either of the poems to read aloud to the others. Remind them to think about the sound and meaning of individual words and phrases.

Reflect

If the children read both poems, take a vote on which one they prefer. Encourage them to refer back to the poems when giving reasons for their preference.

Challenge

Discuss whether children prefer rhyming or non-rhyming poems. Ensure they give reasons for their answers.

Follow-up

PCM 6 *Who Says a Poem Always Has to Rhyme?*: Writing.
Challenge Children could write their own poem of favourite words using *Some Favourite Words* as a model.

Lesson 12

Think

Ask the children to recap some of the features of poems that are good for reading aloud, such as catchy rhymes, funny-sounding words or onomatopoeia, a strong rhythm. Ask them to think of any playground rhymes they know by heart. Playground rhymes are part of the 'oral tradition', passed down through generations. Children may know different variations of the same basic rhyme.

Read and Respond

Read together the page of playground rhymes in the anthology and discuss them with the children.

> The following questions can be used as prompts:
> - Which of these rhymes are familiar and which are new?
> - Are they funny or serious? *They are all light-hearted and humorous.*
> - What else do they all have in common? *They have a strong, regular rhythm and catchy rhymes.*
> - Why do you think a good rhythm is important for a playground rhyme? *Because they are used for skipping or ball-bouncing and the rhythm helps you to keep going.*

Going Deeper

Talk about why the rhymes appeal and what creates the humour in each. For example:
- *Beelzabub (a wonderful word to say aloud) is a name for the devil, but the poem itself describes him as a "jolly old man".*
- *A squashed peanut turning into peanut butter.*
- *The quick fire comebacks in* See You Later, Alligator.
- *The out-of-character actions of the bean-eating judge and his submarine-shooting wife.*

Challenge
How many of the rhymes can the children learn by heart by the end of the session? Pupils could be paired for this activity.

Reflect

Which rhyme did individual children like best? What appealed to them about this rhyme? Which is the favourite rhyme overall?

Challenge
What other kinds of texts have been handed down through generations? *Myths, fables, legends, fairytales.*

Follow-up

No PCM Write your own version of *Order in the Court* by replacing the word "bean" at the end of line 2 and the words "shooting submarines" at the end of line 4.

Challenge Write your own playground rhyme using any of the poems read as a model.

Poems

- Playground rhymes (p. 23)

Key Teaching Objectives

Y3 Strand 1: 3 Sustain conversation, explain or give reasons for their views or choices

Y3 Strand 7: 3 Identify how different texts are organised

Y3 Strand 7: 5 Explore how different texts appeal to readers using varied sentence structures and descriptive language

Y3 Strand 8: 1 Share and compare reasons for reading preferences

Y3 Strand 8: 3 Identify features that writers use to provoke readers' reactions

At a Glance

Playground rhymes are part of the 'oral tradition', like traditional stories. And like traditional stories, they often have slight variations.

Children may well already be familiar with the playground rhymes in this anthology, but may not have seen them written down. On the page, they are able to explore their structure and rhyme patterns.

One of the main characteristics of playground rhymes is a strong rhythm, because they are often used to accompany actions such as skipping and ball-bouncing. Children can identify the rhythms in these rhymes (clapping the rhythm is an effective strategy) and look for patterns of sounds (like rhyme) that create effects.

As the rhymes are short and catchy, they are ideal for learning by heart.

Name: _____ **Date:** _____

Jellyfish Stew

Read *Jellyfish Stew* (page 18) carefully, and then answer the questions on another sheet of paper.

You can find some of the answers in the poem. For others, you will need to work out the answer from clues in the poem, or use your own experience to guess at an answer. And for others you will need to give your own opinion about the poem.

1. What do you think the poet likes about jellyfish stew?

2. Find a word that rhymes with *"noodles"*. What does the word mean?

3. Which words rhyme with *"stew"* in the first verse?

4. Find three words which help you to imagine what it would feel like to eat jellyfish.

5. What would the poet do in exchange for one oozy spoonful?

6. What do you think makes jellyfish stew *"creepy to see"*?

7. Make a list of all the *"oo"* sounds you can find in the second verse.

8. Choose your favourite line. Explain why you like it.

9. What makes this a good poem for reading aloud?

PCM 5

Jellyfish Stew
Skills: Literal, inferential and evaluative comprehension

Name: _____ **Date:** _____

How Can I? (page 16)

❶ This poem is made up of lots of everyday sayings. If you take them literally, they sound crazy! Make a list, and explain what each one really means. For example, to *wind up* means to *annoy*.

❷ Think of some more sayings to add new verses to the poem. For example, *pull myself together, hold my tongue, drive you round the bend, bottle up my feelings*. Start the first line of the verse with "*How can I …*" and the second line with "*When …*"

Animal riddle (page 17)

Animal riddle makes a good model for you to imitate. Think of the animal you want to write about. Write its name in capital letters down the middle of the page. Think about what your animal looks like, how it moves, and what it does. Write down your ideas on another bit of paper. Then try and fit the words around the name, as the poet has done in his poem.

Who Says a Poem Always Has to Rhyme? (page 22)

This poem takes you by surprise because you expect a rhyme. Think of a well-known nursery rhyme and give it the same treatment. For example:

Humpty Dumpty sat on a…*
Humpty Dumpty had a great…**

*rocking horse **grandma

How Can I?, Animal Riddle and Who Says a Poem Always Has to Rhyme?

Skill: Using poem as model for creating and shaping own text

WRITING PCM 6

Rigby
Halley Court, Jordan Hill, Oxford, OX2 8EJ
Rigby is an imprint of Pearson Education Limited, a company incorporated in England
and Wales, having its registered office at Edinburgh Gate, Harlow, Essex, CM20 2JE.
Registered company number: 872828

www.rigbyed.co.uk

Rigby is a registered trademark of Reed Elsevier, Inc, licensed to Pearson Education Limited

© Chris Buckton and Pearson Education Ltd 2008

First published 2008

The Snake's Pyjamas Teaching Notes   ISBN 978 0 433011 94 1
The Snake's Pyjamas 6 pack
with Teaching Notes   ISBN 978 0 433011 22 4

12 11 10 09 08
10 9 8 7 6 5 4 3 2 1

All rights reserved. The material in this publication is copyright. Pupil sheets may be
freely photocopied for classroom use in the purchasing institution. However, this material
is copyright and under no circumstances may copies be offered for sale. If you wish to
use the material in any way other than that specified you must apply in writing to the
publishers.

Series Editors for original version: Chris Buckton, Jean Kendall and Alison Price
Original teaching notes written by Chris Buckton
This version written by Gina Nuttall
Cover illustration by Paul Hess
Logo artwork by Max Ellis
Typeset by Planman Technologies, India
Printed and bound in the UK by Ashford Colour Press